# MAINE

## The Pine Tree State

### BY
### JOHN HAMILTON

**Abdo & Daughters**

An imprint of Abdo Publishing | abdopublishing.com

**abdopublishing.com**

Published by ABDO Publishing, a division of ABDO, PO Box 398166, Minneapolis, Minnesota 55439. Copyright © 2017 by Abdo Consulting Group, Inc. International copyrights reserved in all countries. No part of this book may be reproduced in any form without written permission from the publisher. ABDO & Daughters™ is a trademark and logo of ABDO Publishing.

Printed in the United States of America, North Mankato, Minnesota.
022016
092016

THIS BOOK CONTAINS
RECYCLED MATERIALS

**Editor:** Sue Hamilton       **Contributing Editor:** Bridget O'Brien
**Graphic Design:** Sue Hamilton
**Cover Art Direction:** Candice Keimig       **Cover Photo Selection:** Neil Klinepier
**Cover Photo:** iStock
**Interior Images:** Alamy, Amtrak, AP, Dreamstime, Getty, History in Full Color-Restoration/Colorization, iStock, Library of Congress, L.L. Bean, Maine Black Bears, Maine Historical Society, Maine Secretary of State, Mile High Maps, Minden Pictures, Mountain High Maps, National Portrait Gallery/Smithsonian Institution, New York Public Library, Nike, North Wind Picture Archives, One Mile Up, Portland Pirates, Portland Sea Dogs, Science Source, U.S. Forestry Service, U.S. Navy, Wark Photography, Wikimedia.

**Statistics:** *State and City Populations*, U.S. Census Bureau, July 1, 2014 estimates; *Land and Water Area*, U.S. Census Bureau, 2010 Census, MAF/TIGER database; *State Temperature Extremes*, NOAA National Climatic Data Center; *Climatology and Average Annual Precipitation*, NOAA National Climatic Data Center, 1980-2015 statewide averages; *State Highest and Lowest Points*, NOAA National Geodetic Survey.

**Websites:** To learn more about the United States, visit booklinks.abdopublishing.com. These links are routinely monitored and updated to provide the most current information available.

### Cataloging-in-Publication Data

Names: Hamilton, John, 1959- author.
Title: Maine / by John Hamilton.
Description: Minneapolis, MN : Abdo Publishing, [2017] | Series: The United
    States of America | Includes index.
Identifiers: LCCN 2015957608 | ISBN 9781680783216 (lib. bdg.) |
    ISBN 9781680774252 (ebook)
Subjects: LCSH: Maine--Juvenile literature.
Classification: DDC 974.1--dc23
LC record available at http://lccn.loc.gov/2015957608

# CONTENTS

# THE PINE TREE STATE

**W**hen dawn breaks over the United States, the first rays of sunlight fall upon the craggy coast of Maine. The state is treasured for its rugged landscape, from thick forests and rolling mountains to a coastline that hides deep, protected bays and coves. Just off the mainland, the Atlantic Ocean is sprinkled with hundreds of rocky islands. Many of them are home to fishing boats or summer guests.

People from all over the country flock to Maine to enjoy such treasures as Acadia National Park and the state's many charming coastal towns. Maine is also famous for its fish and tasty lobsters.

Maine is called the "Pine Tree State" because of the vast forests that cover most of its land. Logging and shipbuilding began in Maine in the 1600s. The state's outdoor resources are still important today, although they are carefully managed for future generations to enjoy.

*A Maine lobsterman shows off his catch of the day. The state is famous for its tasty lobsters.*

Portland Head Light was first lit on January 10, 1791. It stands today as part of Fort Williams Park, near the town of Cape Elizabeth, Maine.

# QUICK FACTS

**Name:** There is no clear answer about the origin of the state's name. Many people believe it is a sailing reference to the "mainland."

**State Capital:** Augusta, population 18,705

**Date of Statehood:** March 15, 1820 (23rd state)

**Population:** 1,330,089 (41st-most populous state)

**Area (Total Land and Water):** 35,380 square miles (91,634 sq km), 39th-largest state

**Largest City:** Portland, population 66,666

**Nickname:** The Pine Tree State

**Motto:** *Dirigo* (I lead.)

**State Bird:** Black-Capped Chickadee

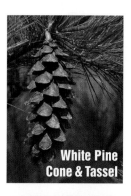

White Pine Cone & Tassel

**State Flower:** White Pine Cone and Tassel

**State Gemstone:** Tourmaline

**State Tree:** White Pine

**State Song:** "State of Maine Song"

Tourmaline

**Highest Point:** Mount Katahdin, 5,268 feet (1,606 m)

**Lowest Point:** Atlantic Ocean, 0 feet (0 m)

Mount Katahdin

**Average July High Temperature:** 77°F (25°C)

**Record High Temperature:** 105°F (41°C), in North Bridgton on July 4 and 10, 1911

**Average January Low Temperature:** 4°F (-16°C)

Atlantic Ocean

**Record Low Temperature:** -50°F (-46°C), at Big Black River, on January 16, 2009

**Average Annual Precipitation:** 45 inches (114 cm)

**Number of U.S. Senators:** 2

**Number of U.S. Representatives:** 2

**U.S. Postal Service Abbreviation:** ME

# GEOGRAPHY

Maine is located in the northeastern corner of the United States. Of the six New England states, Maine is the biggest by far. Its land covers 35,380 square miles (91,634 sq km). Despite its size, it is the least-densely populated state east of the Mississippi River. Most people live along the southern coast.

Maine is the easternmost state in the contiguous United States. It shares a border with New Hampshire to the west. To the southeast is the Gulf of Maine, a gulf of the Atlantic Ocean. The Canadian province of New Brunswick is to the north and northeast. To the northwest is the Canadian province of Quebec.

*Most residents of Maine live along the state's beautiful coastline.*

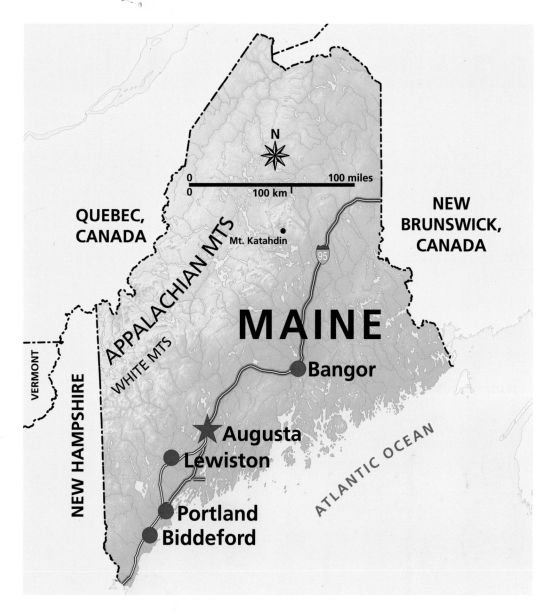

QUEBEC,
CANADA

NEW
BRUNSWICK,
CANADA

N

0                100 miles
0       100 km

Mt. Katahdin

95

APPALACHIAN MTS

WHITE MTS

VERMONT

NEW HAMPSHIRE

**MAINE**

**Bangor**

★ **Augusta**
**Lewiston**

ATLANTIC OCEAN

**Portland**
**Biddeford**

Maine's total land and water area is
35,380 square miles (91,634 sq km).
It is the 39th-largest state. The state
capital is Augusta.

Maine's interior is filled with dense forests, lakes, streams, and bogs. In the northwestern part of the state are the Appalachian Mountains. The rugged White Mountains are part of the Appalachians.

Thousands of years ago, Ice Age glaciers scoured the land and carved deep valleys. When the great ice sheets melted, they left behind many lakes.

In 1959, Maine lawmakers named all the mountains in the state the Longfellow Mountains, in honor of the famous Maine-born poet, Henry Wadsworth Longfellow. Most geographers, however, consider Maine's mountains to be an extension of the Appalachian Mountains. Maine's highest point is Mount Katahdin, in the north-central part of the state. It rises 5,268 feet (1,606 m) above sea level.

*Mount Katahdin*

*Several islands are visible from Cadillac Mountain on Maine's Mount Desert Island. The largest of Maine's more than 3,000 islands, Mount Desert Island is a popular tourist destination. Half the island is occupied by Acadia National Park.*

The Aroostook Plateau in northern Maine is one of the few regions suitable for large-scale farming. The state's famous potatoes are grown here.

Maine's Coastal Lowlands are an example of a "drowned coast." When melting Ice Age glaciers caused sea levels to rise thousands of years ago, valleys became bays. Many of Maine's more than 3,000 islands are actually the tops of hills surrounded by the risen sea. The largest is Mount Desert Island, half of which is occupied by Acadia National Park.

Maine is a paddler's paradise. It contains more than 6,000 lakes and thousands of miles of rivers and streams. If straightened into a single line, Maine's coast would measure more than 3,500 miles (5,633 km) long.

# CLIMATE AND
# WEATHER

**M**aine has a humid continental climate. It has warm, mild summers. July's average high temperature is just 77°F (25°C). The record high temperature was 105°F (41°C), in the southwestern town of North Bridgton, on July 4 and 10, 1911.

Winter weather in Maine can be harsh. The average January low temperature is 4°F (-16°C). The lowest temperature ever recorded in Maine occurred on January 16, 2009, on the Big Black River, near the Canadian border. That day, the thermometer sank to a bone-chilling -50°F (-46°C).

Maine's coastal areas are milder in winter, thanks to the Atlantic Ocean. Further inland, however, it is much colder, with more snow. Blizzards sometimes strike the state.

*People in Portland, Maine, make their way through a heavy snowstorm.*

A lightning strike north of Mackworth Island near Portland, Maine.

During the summer, thunderstorms can rumble into Maine, but tornadoes are rare. Nor'easters sometimes bring high winds and downpours in the autumn and winter. Tropical hurricanes also sometimes blow into Maine. By the time they have traveled that far north, they have usually weakened. However, they can still be very dangerous.

## CLIMATE AND WEATHER

# PLANTS AND
# ANIMALS

Maine is famous for its dense forests of white and red pine. In fact, about 89 percent of the Pine Tree State is forestland. Other common trees found in Maine include aspen, maple, spruce, balsam fir, birch, ash, and several species of oak. The official state tree is the white pine. The official state flower is the white pine cone and tassel.

Many of the state's maple trees are tapped to harvest syrup. In recent years, Maine's syrup industry has produced more than 545,000 gallons (2 million liters) of syrup per year, almost enough to fill an Olympic-size swimming pool. Maine is one of the top maple syrup producers in the nation.

**White Mountains National Forest**

Violets

Lady's Slipper

Wild Blueberries

Common Maine wildflowers include purple violets, columbines, tiger lilies, goldenrods, mayflowers, Queen Anne's lace, and lady's slippers. The official state berry is the blueberry. Maine's wild blueberries are harvested by hand from late July to early fall. These tasty, healthy treats are used in everything from pancakes to muffins, or simply eaten by the handful.

Moose

Maine's official state animal is the moose. They are very common in the state's forests and wetlands. These mammals are the largest members of the deer family. An adult male can weigh more than 1,400 pounds (635 km) and stand 6 feet (1.8 m) tall, with an antler spread of 5 feet (1.5 m) or more.

Maine's forests are filled with many other kinds of animals. They include black bears, bobcats, rabbits, white-tailed deer, raccoons, foxes, lynx, martins, minks, muskrats, snowshoe hare, woodchucks, and many more.

With its many forests and wetlands, Maine is home to dozens of species of birds. Common birds found in the state include cardinals, cormorants, cranes, puffins, eagles, falcons, loons, Canada geese, herons, sandpipers, terns, wrens, and many more. The official state bird is the black-capped chickadee. The dainty, five-inch (13-cm) birds are easily identified by their *fee-bee* call, or buzzy *chick-a-dee-dee-dee*.

Lurking beneath Maine's lakes and streams are bass, trout, pike, perch, muskellunge, sunfish, and more. Landlocked salmon is the official state fish. Swimming in the Atlantic Ocean are striped bass, bluefish, mackerel, and bluefin tuna. Maine is famous for its lobsters.

Large sea mammals are often spotted off Maine's rocky coast. They include finback, humpback, minke, and pilot whales, plus orcas, porpoises, dolphins, and seals.

**Puffin**

# HISTORY

The first people to live in today's Maine were Paleo-Indians. These hunter-gatherers arrived between 13,000 and 11,000 years ago. The Red Paint people lived in Maine about 5,000 years ago. They used red clay to line their graves and paint their tools.

Maine's earliest Algonquian-speaking Native American tribes, such as the Micmacs and Abnakis, lived in villages. They hunted, fished, and grew crops on the land.

Groups of Vikings may have explored the coast of Maine around 1000 AD. Many historians, however, don't believe that Vikings were ever in Maine.

In 1498, Italian explorer John Cabot may have landed on the Maine coast. He was exploring North America for England's King Henry VII.

A replica of the Virginia of Sagadahoc.

Nobody is sure, however, if Cabot actually set foot in Maine.

In 1604, the first European settlement in Maine was built by French colonists on Saint Croix Island, but it failed. In 1607, George Popham of England built a colony at the mouth of the Kennebec River. It was soon abandoned because of Maine's harsh winters. Some of the colonists returned home in a ship named *Virginia of Sagadahoc*. It was probably the first European-style ship built in America.

Paleo-Indian hunters in Maine.

Colonists and missionaries from France continued trying to settle Maine in the early 1600s. The French clashed with people from England, who were also trying to settle the area. In 1613, the English destroyed a French Jesuit mission on Mount Desert Island. The borderline between French and English settlements was contested for many years. Harsh weather and Native American raids also made it difficult to settle Maine.

The Plymouth Council for New England was an English stock company. It awarded royal charters, which gave permission to settle land along the north coast of North America. In 1622, it awarded a large part of coastal New England to two men, Sir Ferdinando Gorges and Captain John Mason. In 1629, the pair split their land in two.

Sir Gorges claimed the land east of the Piscataqua River, which became the province of Maine.

Settlements soon sprang up along the coast. They were filled with fishermen, traders, and loggers. The colonists traded with friendly Native Americans. Tragically, many of the Native Americans caught diseases such as smallpox and measles. They had no natural immunity. Many died. Others fled to lands farther west.

In 1652, Maine became a part of Massachusetts. It was ruled by its neighbor to the south until March 15, 1820, when Maine became the 23rd state in the Union. In 1842, the Webster-Ashburton Treaty between the United States and Canada set Maine's official border.

French missionaries come ashore in Somes Sound, Mount Desert Island, Maine.

Before the Civil War (1861-1865), most people in Maine hated slavery. Author Harriet Beecher Stowe wrote her classic anti-slavery novel *Uncle Tom's Cabin* when she lived in Brunswick, Maine. When war broke out in 1861, about 70,000 Mainers joined the Union army and navy. Many fought at major battles such as Gettysburg and the First Battle of Bull Run. More than 9,000 lost their lives.

After the Civil War ended in 1865, Maine's economy bounced back, thanks to its natural resources. In the late 1800s, Maine began using its many rivers to produce hydroelectric energy, which was used to power new factories. Railroads were also built. They made it easier for businesses to transport products to markets in far-away cities.

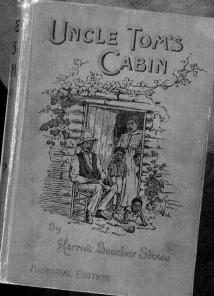

Harriet Beecher Stowe wrote *Uncle Tom's Cabin* when she lived in Maine in the early 1850s. Stowe's story of the horrors of slavery renewed efforts by many Americans to stop people from owning slaves.

*Ships being built at Portsmouth Naval Shipyard's dry dock in Kittery, Maine, in 1908. Congress first approved construction of the 750-foot (229 m) granite dry dock in 1900. The dry dock was built between Fernald's and Seavey's Islands.*

Clothing, paper, and shoemaking businesses grew. The lumber, fishing, and shipbuilding industries continued to be strong. By 1900, approximately half of the country's ships were built in Maine.

The mid-1900s brought many changes to the state. Competition from textile mills in the South forced many Maine textile, clothing, and shoe factories to close. Small, family farms went out of business, and commercial fishing greatly declined due to overfishing. Many shipbuilders went out of business, too. Modern steel vessels no longer needed Maine's sturdy trees.

Today, Maine relies more on service industries and smaller high-tech manufacturing businesses, especially in its busy coastal cities. Tourism has also become a huge industry, boosting Maine's economy.

# DID YOU KNOW?

- Maine is the only state in the contiguous United States that borders just one other state (New Hampshire). It is also the only state with just one syllable in its name.

- The small town of Eastport, Maine, is the first city in the contiguous United States to be struck by the morning light. This easternmost town survives on fishing and tourism.

- The Maine coon is a large, long-haired cat. It is native to the state of Maine, and is one of the country's oldest and largest breeds. Adult males can weigh up to 18 pounds (8 kg). Its origin is a mystery. Tales were once told that it is the result of a normal-sized cat breeding with a raccoon. In reality, it is probably a breed that, over 300 years, has adapted a long fur coat in order to live in Maine's harsh weather. The Maine coon is the official state cat.

**Portland Head Light**

**West Quoddy Head Light**

**Owls Head Light**

- Maine has more than 60 historic lighthouses along its craggy coast.
  Maine's rocky shores and foggy seas were hazardous to early fishing fleets,
  which is why so many lighthouses were built. The oldest lighthouse in
  Maine is Portland Head Light. It is in the southwestern Maine city of
  Cape Elizabeth. It was first lit in 1791, when George Washington was
  president. West Quoddy Head Light, with its red-and-white striped
  tower, marks the easternmost point of the contiguous United States.
  Built in 1858, it guides mariners though the Quoddy Narrows between
  the United States and Canada. Owls Head Light was built in 1825. It is
  located in scenic Owls Head Light State Park, but remains the property
  of the United States Coast Guard. Modern navigation aids have made
  many lighthouses obsolete. Some are now maritime museums.

**DID YOU KNOW?**

# PEOPLE

**Leon Leonwood Bean** (1872-1967) was an inventor, businessman, and outdoorsman. One day, while hunting in the forests of Maine, Bean was annoyed that his boots left him with cold, wet feet. He decided to fix the problem. He designed a pair of lightweight boots with

leather tops and rubber bottoms. The boots were so popular that in 1912 he started a mail-order company called L.L. Bean. His business grew, and he opened his first store. He sold his boots, as well as other sports and outdoor clothing and gear. Today, L.L. Bean's catalog and stores employ nearly 5,000 people worldwide. Leon Bean was born in Greenwood, Maine.

**Stephen King** (1947- ) is an author of some of the scariest horror novels ever written. Many have been made into films. He also writes suspense, fantasy, and science fiction stories. Some of his best-known, terror-filled works include *Carrie*, *Salem's Lot*, *The Shining*, and *The Dark Tower*. The film *The Shawshank Redemption*, based on a novella written by King, was one of the most acclaimed films in modern times. King has sold more than 350 million copies of his books, and has won dozens of awards for his work, including the Bram Stoker Award, the Hugo Award, and the World Fantasy Award. He won the National Medal of Arts in 2015. King was born in Portland, Maine, and has lived in the state for most of his life.

**Milton Bradley** (1836-1911) was an inventor and printer. He developed many famous board games, and founded the Milton Bradley Company in 1860. His first game was *The Checkered Game of Life*, which would later become *The Game of Life*. He believed kids benefited from play. His aim was to make games that were fun and positive. Milton Bradley was born in Vienna, Maine.

**Dorothea Dix** (1802-1887) pioneered the treatment and care of people with mental illness. She was especially active in finding care for poor mentally ill people who could not take care of themselves. She coaxed state governments to build humane mental institutions for the sick and disabled. During the Civil War, Dix was the Union army's superintendent of nurses. She was born in Hampden, Maine.

**Henry Wadsworth Longfellow** (1807-1882) was one of the most popular and acclaimed poets of the 19th century. His poems had a musical quality when read aloud, and told interesting American stories. They are still popular today, and are familiar to most schoolchildren. Some of his best-known poems include "The Song of Hiawatha," "Paul Revere's Ride," and "Evangeline." Longfellow was born in Portland, Maine.

**Joan Benoit Samuelson** (1957- ) won a gold medal at the first women's Olympic marathon race. The history-making contest was held at the 1984 Summer Olympic Games in Los Angeles, California. She also won the Boston Marathon in 1979 and 1981, and the Chicago Marathon in 1985. She held many course time records. After retiring from competitive running, she became a successful coach, author, and race organizer. Samuelson was born in Cape Elizabeth, Maine.

**PEOPLE**

# CITIES

**Augusta** has been the capital of Maine since 1827. Its population is just 18,705, making it one of the smallest state capitals in the country. Augusta is located in the south-central part of the state, about 30 miles (48 km) inland from the coast. The Kennebec River runs through the city. It once produced power for factories and sawmills. Today, important employers include state government, education, health care, retail, transportation, and utilities. The University of Maine at Augusta enrolls about 6,000 students. The Maine State House was built between 1829-1832. It was constructed of granite quarried from the state and hauled to Augusta by oxen.

**Portland** is Maine's largest city. It is on the southwest coast. It has a population of 66,666. It served briefly as the state capital from 1820-1827. During its long history, Portland has burned down four times. The Great Fire of 1866 destroyed 1,500 buildings. It has always been rebuilt, bigger and better than before. Today, Portland is the cultural and business center of the state, thanks in part to its busy port and its closeness to Boston, Massachusetts. Its economy depends on banking, education, health care, and retail shops. Tourism is also very important. The city's famous Arts District boasts many art museums, symphonies, and theaters.

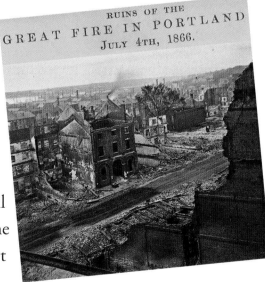

RUINS OF THE GREAT FIRE IN PORTLAND
JULY 4TH, 1866.

**Lewiston** is Maine's second-largest city. Its population is 36,299. Across the Androscoggin River is the city of Auburn, whose population is 22,912. Lewiston and Auburn are sometimes called the "Twin Cities." Lewiston was once a major mill city. Manufacturing has declined, but is still important. The largest employer today is the health care industry, including Central Maine Medical Center and St. Mary's Health System. Other important businesses include retail, education, insurance, and food products. The Lewiston-Auburn area is home to five colleges. Bates College and the University of Southern Maine's Lewiston-Auburn College enroll more than 1,800 undergraduate students combined. Lewiston is home to the Thorncrag Bird Sanctuary. Founded in 1921, it is one of the largest bird sanctuaries in New England.

**Bangor** has a population of 32,568. It is Maine's third-most populous city. It is located in south-central Maine along the Penobscot River. Bangor was once home to large shipyards and sawmills. The Great Fire of 1911 destroyed much of the city, but it was quickly rebuilt using the best materials and building designs of the time. The city remains a showcase of architectural styles. Today, the paper and pulp industries are very important to Bangor's economy. Other major employers include tourism, finance, health care, education, and transportation. A newly revitalized downtown area includes museums, restaurants, art galleries, and bookstores. A 31-foot (9-m) statue of Paul Bunyan highlights the city's lumber industry heritage.

Paul Bunyan

# TRANSPORTATION

The largest commercial airport in Maine is Portland International Jetport. About 1.7 million passengers fly into and out of the airport each year. Other commercial airports in Maine are in Bangor, Augusta, Bar Harbor, Presque Isle, and Rockland.

Maine has eight freight railroads operating in the state on approximately 1,116 miles (1,796 km) of track. The majority of goods hauled are pulp and paper, followed by stone and lumber. Amtrak's Downeaster passenger train runs between Brunswick, Maine, and Boston, Massachusetts. About 560,000 riders take the Downeaster yearly.

About 22,882 miles (36,825 km) of public roadways crisscross Maine. Because of the state's many rivers and streams, there are more than 2,700 bridges. Interstate 95 travels through southwestern Maine, where most of the state's population lives, and then veers northward, heading into New Brunswick, Canada, in the northeastern part of the state.

*The Amtrak Downeaster transports about 560,000 riders each year. The train runs between Brunswick, Maine, and Boston, Massachusetts.*

*The* Queen Mary 2 *sails into Bar Harbor, Mount Desert Island, Maine. The 2,620-passenger, 17-deck ship is the largest ocean liner ever built.*

Each year, ferries shuttle more than 2.1 million passengers and 200,000 vehicles to cities along the coast and to Maine's 15 unbridged year-round inhabited islands. The Port of Portland, in Portland, Maine, is a gateway to the Atlantic Ocean. It is a deepwater port that can handle many ocean-going craft, from luxury cruise ships to massive container vessels. About 12 million tons (10.9 million metric tons) of freight is handled by the port each year. Approximately 100,000 cruise ship passengers visit Portland annually.

## TRANSPORTATION

# NATURAL
# RESOURCES

About 89 percent of Maine's land area is forestland, approximately 17.6 million acres (7.1 million ha). That is almost as much forestland as when Europeans first arrived in the 1600s. Wood products are Maine's top export, representing about $885 million each year. Paper and paperboard are the number one exports, followed by pulpwood and finished wood products. Forestland that is harvested is carefully replanted to benefit future generations.

There are about 8,200 farms in Maine. The total value of Maine's farm products is about $763 million each year. Potatoes are the most valuable crop, especially those grown in fertile Aroostook County in northern Maine. The state leads the world with its wild blueberry harvest. Other important farm products include hay, maple syrup, oats, dairy, eggs, apples, and sweet corn.

*Sap is collected to make maple syrup from about February to April in Maine.*

*Maine's American lobsters can reach great sizes, even up to 3 feet (.9 m) or more in length. However, Maine law requires that a lobster can only be legally taken if its carapace, or body shell, is between 3.25 inches (8.3 cm) and 5 inches (12.7 cm) long. This allows big lobsters to reproduce and small ones to grow up.*

When people think of Maine, many think of lobster. The pure water of the Gulf of Maine gives the lobsters their superior taste. More than 5,600 Maine lobstermen land about 85 percent of the lobsters caught in the United States. Lobster sales add about $1 billion to the state's economy. In addition to lobster, Maine fish farms produce oysters, mussels, and salmon.

## NATURAL RESOURCES

# INDUSTRY

**M**aine is sometimes called "Vacationland." More than 30 million people visit the state each year, making tourism one of Maine's biggest industries. People love Maine's forests, its historic lighthouses, its charming small towns, and its delicious seafood. Tourists spend about $5.4 billion in Maine each year, supporting more than 94,000 jobs. That is about 14 percent of the state's total workforce.

Because Maine is the most forested state in the country, it's no surprise that logging, paper, and wood products are important to the economy. Maine gets an $8 billion boost annually from the forest industry. It supports 39,000 jobs.

A ferry transports passengers past Portland Breakwater Light, also known as "Bug Light," by South Portland, Maine.

*The USS* San Juan, *a Los Angeles-class U.S. Navy submarine, is undocked after routine repairs at the Portsmouth Naval Shipyard in Kittery, Maine.*

Maine has a long history of shipbuilding. The Portsmouth Naval Shipyard is in Kittery, Maine. It repairs and modernizes the country's fleet of nuclear powered submarines. Bath, Maine, is the home of Bath Iron Works. The shipyard designs and builds commercial and military vessels, including Zumwalt-class guided missile destroyers, the most advanced surface warships in the world.

Other important Maine industries include electronics manufacturing, printing, food products, textiles, and leather goods. The outdoor clothing and equipment company L.L. Bean is headquartered in Freeport, Maine.

# SPORTS

Maine has no major league professional sports teams. The Portland Pirates are a minor league professional hockey team. They are an affiliate of the National Hockey League's Florida Panthers. The Portland Sea Dogs are a minor league baseball team. They are an affiliate of Major League Baseball's Boston Red Sox. The Maine Black Bears represent various teams from the University of Maine.

Maine is an outdoor lover's paradise. There are vast wilderness areas to explore, mountain peaks to conquer, and breathtaking seashores to enjoy. The world-famous Appalachian Trail begins in northern Maine, at Mount Katahdin. Hikers can follow the trail south as it winds its way through the state. At Acadia National Park on Mount Desert Island, visitors can camp, hike, or bike as they explore the park's beautiful woods and granite peaks.

*Hikers enjoying the view of Mount Katahdin. The famous Appalachian Trail begins here and ends in the state of Georgia.*

Maine's Bureau of Parks and Lands manages more than 700,000 acres (283,280 ha) of state parks and recreational areas. Outdoor activities include camping, hunting, biking, golfing, horseback riding, rock climbing, and more. For those who like water sports, there are plenty of lakes and rivers for fishing, sailing, kayaking, swimming, and whitewater rafting. In winter, many people put on their parkas and enjoy skiing, snowboarding, ice fishing, snowmobiling, and dog sledding.

# ENTERTAINMENT

**M**ainers love the great outdoors, and their fairs and festivals reflect this. The Great Falls Balloon Festival is held each August in Lewiston. It began in 1992 as a charity event. Today, the festival attracts more than 20 colorful hot air balloons and 100,000 spectators.

The Maine Lobster Festival takes place in August in the coastal town of Rockland. Tens of thousands of visitors come to enjoy five days of cooking contests, entertainers, artists, carnival rides, and, of course, to eat lobster.

**Windjammers sail at the start of the Great Schooner Race, held during Windjammer Days in June in Boothbay Harbor.**

Windjammer Days, in Boothbay Harbor, is a week-long festival held each June. The highlight is a small fleet of square-masted sailing ships. They arrive in the harbor on the second day of the festival. Called windjammers, these large vessels were used in the late 1800s and early 1900s to carry cargo.

Many Maine cities have community theater groups or ballet companies. Mainers love many kinds of music. Both Bangor and Portland have professional orchestras. There are also many jazz, blues, and folk music festivals held throughout the state.

The Maine State Aquarium is in West Boothbay Harbor. It features many fish and invertebrates found lurking in Maine's rivers, lakes, and ocean floor. One exhibit shows off lobsters, including giants weighing up to 23 pounds (10 kg).

# ENTERTAINMENT

# TIMELINE

**11,000-9,000 BC**—The first Paleo-Indians arrive in the Maine area.

**3,000 BC**—The Red Paint People use red clay to line their graves and paint tools. Other Native Americans soon group together in villages.

**1498**—Italian explorer John Cabot may have landed on the Maine coast.

**1604**—First European settlement built in Maine by French colonists on Saint Croix Island. The colony fails.

Fort Popham

**1607**—George Popham of England builds a settlement at the mouth of the Kennebec River.

**1629**—Sir Fernando Gorges receives land east of the Piscataqua River, which eventually becomes the province of Maine.

**1652**—Maine becomes a part of Massachusetts.

**1820**—Maine becomes the 23$^{rd}$ state on March 15. Portland is named as the capital.

**1827**—Maine officially changes the location of its capital to the more centrally located city of Augusta.

**1842**—The Webster-Ashburton Treaty ends a border dispute between Maine and the Canadian province of New Brunswick.

**1861**—The Civil War begins. Maine sends about 70,000 soldiers and sailors to fight for the Union.

**1866**—The Great Fire of 1866 destroys most of downtown Portland, Maine. The city is quickly rebuilt.

**1900s**—Maine's logging, shipbuilding, and fishing industries grow.

**1947**—A terrible forest fire sweeps through Maine coastal communities, destroying hundreds of homes and blackening thousands of acres of forest, including a large part of Acadia National Park.

**1984**—Maine native Joan Benoit Samuelson wins the first-ever Olympic gold medal in the women's marathon event at the Summer Olympic Games in Los Angeles, CA.

**2013**—The USS *Zumwalt* is launched from the Bath Iron Works shipyard in Bath, Maine. It is the first of a new class of stealthy guided missile destroyers.

# GLOSSARY

### ALGONQUIAN

A group of very similar Native American languages. Many of New England's tribes were Algonquian-speaking people, including the Micmacs and Abnakis.

### CARAPACE

The hard upper shell found on crustaceans, such as lobsters, as well as on turtles and arachnids.

### CIVIL WAR

The war fought between America's Northern and Southern states from 1861-1865. The Southern states were for slavery. They wanted to start their own country. Northern states fought against slavery and a division of the country.

### COLONY

A colony is the establishment of a settlement in a new location. It is often ruled by another country.

### GLACIERS

Huge sheets of ice that grow and shrink as the climate changes. They shape the land beneath them.

### HURRICANE

A violent wind storm that begins in tropical ocean waters. Hurricanes cause dangerously high tides and bring deadly waves, driving rain, and even tornados. Hurricanes break up and die down after reaching land.

### HYDROELECTRIC ENERGY

A method of creating electricity from the flowing of water.

### MISSION

A religious settlement or outpost, which usually includes a church and a school.

### NEW ENGLAND

An area in the northeastern United States consisting of six states. It includes Maine, Connecticut, Vermont, New Hampshire, Massachusetts, and Rhode Island.

### NOR'EASTER

A large storm that forms when warm air over the Atlantic Ocean clashes with cold Arctic air blown in from Canada. Nor'easters get their name from the northeasterly direction of their winds. They can be very destructive, but are usually less dangerous than tropical hurricanes.

### PALEO-INDIANS

Prehistoric ancestors of today's Native Americans.

### WEBSTER-ASHBURTON TREATY

An agreement establishing the border between Maine and New Brunswick, Canada. The treaty also established other United States and Canada boundaries. It allowed the United States to use the St. John River, and called for the two countries to work together to stop the slave trade on the African coast. The treaty was created in 1842 by Daniel Webster of the United States and Lord Ashburton of Great Britain. At the time, Great Britain ruled Canada. The treaty ended the possibility of fighting between the countries.

# INDEX